ON TIME

ALSO BY JOANNE KYGER

2012 (Blue Press, 2013)
Lo & Behold (Voices from the American Land, 2009)
Not Veracruz (Libellum Press, 2007)
About Now: Collected Poems (National Poetry Foundation, 2007)
God Never Dies: Poems from Oaxaca (Blue Press, 2013)
As Ever: Selected Poems (Penguin Books, 2002)
Again: Poems 1989–2000 (La Alameda Press, 2001)
Strange Big Moon: The Japan & India Journals (North Atlantic Press, 2000)
Some Life (The Post-Apollo Press, 2000)

ON TIME

Poems 2005–2014

Joanne Kyger

City Lights Books | San Francisco

WATERS 2009 by Arthur Okamura
from the Estate of Arthur Okamura
with permission of Kitty Okamura
Photo: Jane Kleider

Some of these poems have appeared in:
Amerarcana, Court Green, Lars Palm's Ungovernable Press, Mimeo Mimeo, Spoon River Anthology, Bombay Gin, White Wall Review, and *Star 82 Review*

Not Veracruz, Libellum Press
The Distressed Look, Coyote Press
Sore Dove Broadside 2007

Library of Congress Cataloging-in-Publication Data
Kyger, Joanne.
[Poems. Selections]
On time : poems 2005-2014 / Joanne Kyger.
pages ; cm
ISBN 978-0-87286-680-5 (alk. paper)
I. Title.

PS3561.Y35A6 2015
811'.54—dc23

2015001495

City Lights Books are published at the City Lights Bookstore
261 Columbus Avenue, San Francisco, CA 94133
www.citylights.com

DEDICATED TO THE MEMORY OF
ARTHUR OKAMURA
Artist, Teacher, Friend
February 24, 1932–July 10, 2009

"The truly still mind, with which you were born,
is a mind that moves freely.
It reacts wholeheartedly to everything it encounters,
to everything on which it reflects."

—*Soko Morinaga*

from *Novice to Master. An Ongoing Lesson in the Extent of My Own Stupidity.*
Translated by Belenda Attaway Yamakawa. Wisdom Press, 2002.

ON TIME

Sunday

When your "mind" flies
away with a poem on a page, do you both
end up in a lonesome place
in the backyard of words
as soft and familiar as the bee
buzzing the blue glass
which is the only company
you have

Sharp rap in the knee
—a tiny apple falls through gravity

You have a "way" with your words—
"thinking is a pathology"
that has found freshly discovered ground
but if you "think your way
into the next scenarios"
Good luck!
Buster Bush and Co. have whacked the globe
a hard blow of the uglies pathogen
and it's a disastrous scene

Note the tiniest first baby quail
in the far scallop of shadow—

a tender mouthful of hope
scratching down a dainty slope
of wind to move on

July 24, 2005

"You Go to War with the Army You Have"

"The froth of rapid associations"
is entirely in the mind
This "here" is not moving

Our garden has become over run
with a new generation of scrub jays

They make very loud sounds
and fly about aggressively
pecking holes in the apples

To make them fly away we clap our hands
or tap on the window
They mostly learn to shut up

The other day, our friend from Argentina
saw us run out on the deck
after lunch
and clap our hands

He thought it was some kind
of New Age California ritual
to end a meal

Time later to find out
what went right
and what didn't go right, right?

September 2005

Happy New Year

Into the storm tossed year padding
and scudding across the brain
pan of the holidays
—there's my door mat
blown into the bushes

Was Mao really a repellant mass
murderer, an untalented liar
and never brushed his teeth?

John Yoo tells George Bush
there are no laws
that limit
his power—
no laws of war apply.

So when Bush is captured
there's no way he'll have
a painless or legal time
locked up with his holy tostado—
God the Revelator

January 2, 2006

All Night

All night
my neighbor's son was the object
of my dreaming. Towards dawn
he patted my shoulder
in farewell as I ashamed
of my youthful longing
pretended not to care,

Where did you come from kiddo
—Tab Hunter's "Confidential"?
fresh from the library's biographies
& the '50s sexual firewall

A probe blasts off from earth to Pluto
It's getting more violent in Afghanistan

But newly elected in Chile
is the first female president
socialist Michelle Bachelet

Little thicket house of privet
the quail ease in and out of
dust bath in wood chips

Tomorrow will be simple with friends
on a walk to the place
where Bill McNeill's ashes lay
on a cliff
above the sea
As natural as
it's going to be.

January 19, 2006

What the Storms Did

Remember that teenage horror movie
where kids are walking
through the graveyard

And a big hand comes out
of the murky earth
and drags them down
to hell or worse

Well we find Bill's site
split in the middle
by a gash three feet deep
running towards the cliff
and the sea

Can't find any bones or ashes
where Whalen and Dorsey
ceremonially chanted
for a Zen comrade's last feat

Joko, Judy and me
marvel
at the showman he is

Incense smoke and Kannon's beat
NOTHING stops Bill
on his way to the Beach

January 20, 2006
for Bill McNeill

The Studio

Septic tank is full
not working
after all day rain

thrilled with the news?

I need friends from outer space

to save me from knee jerk belligerence
and total lack of coherent thought

Let me look south to the "existence of good"
and the indigenous inheritance of autonomy

"Okay go ahead and do it!"

in this rhetorical exercise

before I again gain the prone
thru the afternoon

and the cliffs slip downward
just like democracy
carrying the pine
and surrounding vegetation

dumped like gangster tactics
on the rocks below

Well, indulging the maintenance
of the thin emotional line of balance
is what I call life these days

See figures in the mist
—an evolution's first steps

February 2006

Targeted Killing

"There are a few countries
where the president has decided
we can 'whack' someone
without approval or knowledge
of the host government".

—former CIA official

February 4, 2006

White Kites

Oh those gorgeous White Kites
 courting in the tops of the pines
 around here they sound

a sweetish dove grey whistle
to each other

February 6, 2006

For a Moment

for a moment
it's agonizing, sad, final

February 8, 2006

So Still

eleven surfers
out there
going nowhere

February 11, 2006

A Record

Thirty one days in the month
Twenty six had rain

U.S. government
radical religion, oil, borrowed money

Good morning
fragments

of last night's travels
in that invisible state called "dream"
sneak around with cardboard boxes
full of old poetry

cold ocean, but few salmon

Everything happened anyway
but not in Veracruz

Quick go out, before it rains.
Several days a week
just lay there and read

Get guilty over listening
to the assurance of news
reporting voices that say
"We're acting in the best interests
for your security, making you 'safe'"

Here with a border just under you
that's totally OPEN

looking more like a cradle
of the heart to come

"What is it that I started
long ago
and how can I get back
to that"
Walt Whitman said
when he wrote
about California

Okay, let the winds blow, let the storms come
the real estate fall off the cliffs
into the sea
banging noisily

It's a test
of the authentic

unborn, beyond

March 31, 2006

Good Friday Slack

Moon white & orange poppies
glow across the way
baring themselves
to the newly minted sun

Better take a break
in case Sean Wilsey
whom I've spent
reading the past two
horribly inclement days
wants to say
a few words

of dedicated angry savagery.
Can you resist him? Am I getting suckered
into believing these social parodies
exist as material for the end of a dick
fighting for a soul?

It's on my mind how the old man died
in Mill Valley Wednesday night
when mud
oozed over him in the rain
as he tried to fix
the drainage behind his house

I was out in boots too
hoisting books in the shed
off the floor
in case flood makes
poetry a sodden remnant

As mud rises over the ankles remember
to cut some Good Friday slack
for your guests

April 13, 2006

"Are You One of Those Revolutionary Poets?"

A small bundle of Lilies of the Valley
marks Worker's Day in Europe

A day when even Patrick Buchanan
gives a stay away
approach to foreign policy
in Iran

I'm sorry the Renku rules
were so hard to grasp
I almost threw
them away

This doesn't happen easily, does it

Slight wind blown
tiny white petal
on the ground

May 1, 2006
for Pat Nolan

Pomegranate Syrup

There's hardly a breeze
moving today
a day when electricity is gone

from this part of town
one can hear
the Duxbury foghorn
and the internal

combustion engine going down
Elm Road
as the breath runs out of Lebanon
like a vast sigh

like a vast sigh
the radio goes silent
only a plane

overhead
sounds ominous

Fifteen feet up
a bamboo top

now bends in a slight wind
This could be

a moment of "trust"
in a time that spells
an arrogant landing
of hellbent despair

"Power may be restored"
in an hour or two

So try this tangy sweet taste
of pomegranate
to wake up   seeds that spring

from the newly born
then torn apart body
of our old and awesome friend Dionysus

whose blood allows these seeds to grow
fruit red and split open like a wound

To resurrect against
"the humiliation and infringement of a sovereignty"

use Punica granatum
a solid wild hedge
for a border.

August 2006

Obligation

I'm trying to find my mother in the gift shop
It's not that I like her very much
      but it's my obligation
            and besides I don't want to be left behind

January 4, 2007

Spending Time

The assiduous comments of an angry inch of quails
    Cleaning up   the Christmas tree's furry needles
        It all becomes Sunday after history

Lost in a book, away into someone else's family
  and landscape absorbed in the sun behind
    the eucalyptus' attentive wave through the window

Is it all even now? The way time spends time?

January 6, 2007

Essentially

The preparation is mostly mental
An inside acrobatics of temperament
It doesn't take long to fall
from a place near the sunset

Meanwhile in Bill's dream salon I shake out
the evening's blankets

and explain to him that his first wife
had moments of sharp clarity
in her poetry—which she hardly ever wrote

Whereupon she immediately emails from Mexico
to thank me

"out in the open
everywhere to go"

Past the Sunday accident
on top of thirteen curves

to the tradition of pithy insults which one adores
even from robins having a sparring match
with each other

the most gracefully dangerous
dance they can do

Last night I murmur "Om Ah Hum"
to explain where syllables
lay in the body

Someone pours beer over themselves

"Your God is a lump of clay, mine is a meteorite"

A conversation ensues
essentially grateful, mostly graceful

January 20, 2007

Morning Train

Morning trains my eye on you
and fades near the rooms of the night
Seconds ago   another drifts in

Survived the April fool
just to feel someone was left

behind in the salvation hall

Why is it violent? This

cross rebirth stuff
on a cannabis screen

still real with the TV turned off

On the other hand
just enjoy the seconds
you can

continue with change
in the moving morning light

April 2, 2007
for Micah Ballard

Elegant Simplicity

or an unrefined step

about entering into an agreement
with the page of the moment

Demons are more or less human in appearance
Monsters are more animal like

The first soul or spirit
that resides in a person is immortal

The second soul is the animal spirit
you acquire at birth
with a real counterpart
animal spirit
roving around in the world.

If it dies, you die
That's it.

May 22, 2007

Monday's Belief

When you look ahead
into a century

the time behind seems solid and finite
and perhaps "knowable"

I could have stamped my feet with fury

to find all so thusly crammed
into a human head
of knowledge
which allows such shambles
of articulation

to be cut short. Don't answer the phone
We are not at home.

June 18, 2007

Summer Solstice

"I have to go downtown now
because the buckeye blossoms
are in my eye
making me cry"

We have six buildings in our compound
The tallest and oldest
is the headquarters
It has the plumbing

Much less restless
than when I moved to this spot
36 years ago
Never thought
it would be so pleasant

And stable to hear crows
battle in the pine across the road
tomorrow

June 21, 2007

Myokyo Dream

"Stop fidgeting" she says
I'm picking candle wax off my robes
We're all sitting in the Zendo
People of all ages introducing themselves.

"I'm here because I read too much" I say.

—Zengetsu Myokyo is Abbot of Empukuji,
the Montreal Zen Center.
Joshu Sasaki, her teacher, is 100 years old
and has never written a book.

August 4, 2007

Left of the Black Line

One two three four five six

Sifting the ashes of the household
incense burners

"May incense fragrance benefit us all"
How could that be?
Respect and honor for the deity

that sniffs the fumes above
"Ah they're thinking of me"

As smoke rises
one looks up
to a new roof
with gratitude
although a pain in the ass
all that time spent
on doodles of the domestic

Where else would you dwell?
Under a government umbrella?

"What we call American Democracy
will likely be
a casualty of hypocrisy"

August 25, 2007

Permission by the Horns

"It's true, as Duncan used to say,
We need permission for what we do
Next we must grab permission by the horns & hang on

It isn't just a rant, a gift, a boon. Grab it and run
Before they change their minds."

—*Philip Whalen*
"*Treading Water,*" 1978

I

The mocking bird nearby is perfectly replicating the quail's
three note descending call

Time to move the ashes
back to the main house
Bits of my friends
Nancy, Philip, and quite remorselessly
ashes I can no longer identify
Planning to put them in the ground
under a large rock.
Which isn't there yet.

Writing poems, at the beginning, was a place to put
some untidy emotions.
Until I realized
nobody wanted to read about them.

This sounds like a simple improvisation
but actually it's composed

To the cemetery on the Day of the Dead with marigolds
One for each grave that we know, and one for the old old ones

Vincente Fox, the last president of Mexico, says in his memoir
that George Bush walks
like he has a watermelon under each arm

Sunday morning rain,   oil spill still moving,   along the shore

"European Parliament last week proposed
turning the Afghanistan poppy crop
into legal opium based painkillers"

Impatient with the young local's posturing of "entitlement"

II

In the poet's hut
a cool lay back
watching the red current bloom
gracefully

recumbent

Fox, I know those two little piles of shit
left on the outdoor table
are yours.

She understood that obstacles could be removed
if their illusory state was realized
in the moment.

Circle of seven men standing, outdoors, all eating asparagus.

Thank god I don't write Everything down

The stupider I thought you were
the more I had to learn

Formulas, prayers, rituals passed down
by word of mouth
5,000 years ago
to know what you know now

Everything gone, changed, unfamiliar
This is a dreadful nightmare
Where is my round table, my little white desk

We already miss you
eight days later

It's true
hope can cause pain

Spring 2008

The Olympic Torch in San Francisco

They drove out of town to the airport
the torch between their legs

The protection
protected the runners
so much you couldn't see them
as they dodged around town to avoid those
who wanted to say something fierce

Just think of the expense to keep them "safe"
Local police, State police, and the Chinese police
who were ready to snatch even the tiniest Tibetan flag
out of a runner's hand
and drag her out of the race
(I had another one up my sleeve, she said)

April 9, 2008

The Art of Living Slowly

How I wish I had had
my hair cut before being photographed
at the local Figure Drawing show
last Saturday which will live

on the front page of the weekly Coastal News
for as long as paper and air last

And may I ask
how old is air?
Holding the sorrowful remnants of little nations
who conquered littler nations
whose names we don't even know any more
although the ground remains
the same in patient aging
or you can drop the patient part
this ground is changing, always changing

April 11, 2008

Summer Sorting

It's amazing how articulate you can be
without any idea of what you are saying

Lots of hair tearing and vocalizations

Is "failure" a fake judgement?

One hears the nation needs "energy" "growth"
What about "repose"

                    It takes about five minutes
        for graciousness to set in

Keep aiming for simplicity of thought
Unless, of course, you like overabundance

Assume the world's wealth is in pebbles and leaves
        freely laying there
          on the ground

Summer 2008

Fact Checking

In 1962 when I was leaving India with Gary Snyder
I saw a necklace, called a "beggars necklace"
made of semi precious stones that I wanted
Gary said, yes you can buy it
 if you learn the real names of all the stones
(never pass up an opportunity for self education)

The *New Yorker* magazine is doing a profile of Snyder
and I told the reporter, Dana Goodyear, this story
and showed her the necklace.

A *New Yorker* fact checker, Chris Jennings, called me up yesterday
and wanted to know
how many different stones there were in the necklace
Dana wrote that there were "dozens"
I went and got the necklace and counted the different kinds of stones
over the phone to the fact checker
Eight. Different kinds of stones

Red, orange, green, milky white, blue
mossy green, mottled brown, glittery rust.

September 17, 2008

Bottoms Up

A very stable negativity
Do not despair for at least another five minutes

While you take a break to feed your demons
—a very complicated piece of cooking

but worth it for the world
is starting to seem other than it is

An exhausted song sparrow has just arrived
from the north

starting to locate
some ease
into this space

The season's first rain is gentle
and all day long

September 21, 2008

Poetic Perfection

Is the Culmination of All Wisdom and Beauty

Are you recognizing this for what it is?

ELEMENTAL UNIVERSAL
and even bigger than this—a trillion times

(like the national debt)

ENORMOUS TREMENDOUS

open wide
say
AH!

October 2008

Trying the New Year 2009

You have to give EVERYTHING you have

ALL OF THE TIME
not just some of the time

Put everything you have into it
and then go outside and rest

It's fear or pain that drives one to quit
those tiresome addictions
and this so called "strength"

of character blooms like a lotus
in the muddy footprints
of the past

A sick feeling
that the boredom of repetition
might be over

It's three o'clock

January 2, 2009

Iron Fist

Do you really think an "enemy" can be "killed"?
Do you think the enemy will ever go away
as long as it still inhabits that entity called "enemy"?

"Stopping the offensive now
would waste the great strides
this country has made
with the iron fist of the people
in a fight to the bitter end."

Meanwhile the sinister weather of summer
has entered the winter month of January
—there is a dawning awareness
that the "system" has crashed.

January 7, 2009

Seventy-Seven
Beautiful and Adorable Things
for Arthur Okamura's 77Th Birthday

1. A very beautiful thing is the clay cup from your Kyushu family
2. An adorable thing is the face of a child you have drawn on a melon in the garden
3. or King Charles Charley sleeping on his back
4. Simply beautiful is the great blue heron trying to get into
   your tightly guarded fish pond
5. and the way you draw Einstein
6. and the way you draw yourself
7. and the way your draw all those naked ladies
8. An especially beautiful thing is watching you play ping pong on TV
   after you have eaten one of Margot Doss's brownies
9. Both adorable and beautiful is when you draw from the right side of your brain
10. and doze on the right side of your brain
11. and take a shower with the right side of your brain
12. and drive a car with the right side of your brain
13. Those quail eggs are simple and beautiful
14. as are Kitty's decorations at Christmas
15. Barack Obama's lips are very adorable when you mold them in Play-Doh
16. Quite beautiful is Ryoan-ji's classic stone garden
17. and your painterly appreciation of it
18. Disgustingly un-adorable is Dick Cheney on TV

19. and George Bush falling off his mountain bike
20. and falling off his couch all by himself watching the Superbowl
21. and getting a bruise on his face
22. Refreshingly beautiful is a clear morning after heavy rain
23. when you wear your vest of silk
24. and make a perfect pot of rice
25. and a monarch butterfly nonchalantly flies through the open door
26. and lands on top of your pen while you draw
27. Beautiful and adorable things that you never paint are unicorns
    and cherry blossoms
28. Sometimes adorable are the flowering tree dahlias which have taken over
    your garden
29. but never need to be watered
30. It is beautiful when much praise for insights are given
31. especially when they are yours and you just made them up on the spot
32. Really beautiful is a Bob Creeley poem you haven't ever seen before
    that mentions you by name
33. or when someone compares you to Rembrandt
34. or refers to you as the Michelangelo of Bolinas
35. You have a bad dream and consult a dream interpreter
    who tells you the dream is actually beautiful
36. Hilary Clinton visiting in town is holding forth about a recent event—
    several people stand near her, but it is you she keeps looking at as she
    speaks

37. You've lost something, start to look for it, and find it right under your nose
38. Someone gives you drawing paper of very fine quality made in Belgium
and you immediately do a charming drawing of Charley's profile
39. which the neighbor's envious dog then tries to pee on
40. It is both beautiful and adorable that you can turn yourself into a rabbit
and pull yourself out of a top hat you have just drawn
41. And it is both beautiful and adorable when you "cluck" your friends under the chin
42. and impressively beautiful when you skip rocks along the lagoon channel
43. and jump from a standing position onto the bar at Smiley's
44. and play the saxophone under almost any conditions
45. including when the saxophone is made of sea kelp
46. and play a game of cribbage
47. and make heavenly barbecue pork
48. and carve radishes into roses
49. It is exceptionally adorable to watch Charley's large eyes
and total poker face and wonder what he is thinking about
or if he is thinking at all
50. It is also adorable when you take a pair of scissors and cut out
one of those little men
51. you know, the one whose penis waves up and down
52. and when you ask someone to draw three trees, a road, and a fence
and you read their entire life history from the drawing

53. It is plaintively beautiful when you make a paper airplane out of a $100 bill
and it flies out the window
54. and it doesn't even bother you
55. because you know it's not really real
56. And it is really adorable when you make rings out of US currency
that people can wear on their fingers in case of emergencies
57. And of course it is totally adorable when you pull out your pipe and offer a toke
58. but you never show the effects
59. because you are using both sides of your brain simultaneously
60. while painting a picture of Marilyn Monroe upside down
61. It is very beautiful that you can take the *San Francisco Chronicle*
and turn it into a tree
62. or a tropical fish
63. or a very large star
64. Mostly it is terrifically beautiful and adorable that you are a perfect being
65. because perfection is in the eye of the beholder
66. and you have taught us to use our eyes
67. and you have taught us to use the right side of our brain
68. and the left side of our brain
69. as you are one of the brainiest painters
70. who ever lived
71. and so our eyes
72. are beholden
73. to your inventions

74. and terrific use of color
75. to transform air
76. into this birthday celebration
77. for without You we would have nothing to have a beautiful and adorable party about

February 4, 2009
way way after Sei Shonagon
at Michael Lerner's house

Easter

One sees the “stages” of this death
this staggering death, of this “sacrifice”
And then it’s over
and a mysterious reappearance occurs

You again? Forget those tears
We’re in a brand new kingdom
and the reappeared one
is seated on a charming throne

Right next to the Big One
the Almighty Head of State

We’re so happy this was all done for “us”
that we celebrate
this entire drama
every year

and get pissed off all over again

April 10, 2009

Really There Is No Solution

No such thing as a "solution"   it's just going to live on
with one rotten moment after another
until the "situation" wears out and god gets his way
and deeds all land for eternity
to the loudest voice

You know what? this isn't even my business, isn't even
in my back yard. The radio, the TV, the internet, the paper,
brings me all this news that's none of my business
I'm tired of global awareness emanating from my position
at the on and off button

which is now "off"
on the Afghanistan ghastly goal of
"finishing" the "job"

All that "in the moment" stuff—
the rotten moment lives forever
in a very deep pit you can never climb out of

Better shift to some other conceits—
"I go way back, I'm a goddess"

The tall votive candle for Lenore
goes out with a pop as her friends Jim and Maggie
are leaving

"I was born old"
that's why old things are so familiar
like the return of the now ever present mocking bird

Take it easy, when you return, don't let anger mar your entrance

think about your dreams, the comings and goings of people
near the beach, waiting in line
why are you feeling better now…

November 2009

January 1, 2010

A light day rain over
the full moon now
on the other side
of the world

January 2, 2010

No differentiation walk on
cliff path
some of it mud deer trail

"A Minimal Structural Statement of One's Experience"

Wake up bright, from last night's

dreams of many rooms all actively complicated with people
everyone trying to talk through a gauzy mask called "soul"
the dreamer wants to find the wild gods roaming not so far away
—the unavoidable gods
building roads into tomorrow

Sudden rogue waves of January's north coast
take two women   two weeks apart

Sudden rogue waves take the women out to sea
and they are never seen again.
they didn't know each other

Wild iris have started to bloom

Dream towards morning a destination is reached
after a hard night of travel
along a narrow winding road
the wind dies down but clouds shroud the sunrise
and soon block it out

On the other side of the road
the huge surge of the ocean makes an enormous commotion
inside the commotion
the whole history of sea
every note it's ever made

At the cross roads
of fact and imagination
without overstatement
without fantasy

January 20, 2010
Sylvia and Katherine

Drop Stitch for a Chat

It's all right to feel glum while cooking the oyster stew

Are you enjoying this state of mind?
this heaving of ancient emotions
or do they need to be outsourced
and privatized

Carefully diplomatic
one tries to avoid overweight
careless power

Like trying to build a swimming pool next to the ocean
An insane urban desire for exercise
in drinking water

Well that was a waste of a golden moment

January 8, 2010

2010 Gold Tiger Year

Now I'm stuck in here with the awareness

of the yellow jacket flying around
who is bound to expire
once I close the door and exit.

Sulking along the edge of rage
for the rest of your days
"I won't have it!"

Wild, dangerous, extravagant and bright
Big, bold, and unpredictable

SMASH SMASH SMASH SMASH

SHATTER CRASH CRASH CRASH

February 2010

Arthur's Birthday 2010

Now light a small
    red votive
        in front of the photo

of your concentrated drawing
    of what's in front of you

        —the people that miss you.

March 3, 2010
Arthur Okamura
February 24, 1932–July 10, 2009

I'm Very Busy Now
So I Can't Answer All Those Questions
About Beat Women Poets

A startled melancholy underlies all
—the party's over for the dollar

"Blood splattered wall paper
would find a substantial niche market"

Is it that you don't "want" to do it
or is it that you "can't" make

the private public
like the poet

But does the "public"
want to hear it?

U.S. has a lot of enemies
Are they mine too?

—Not a very nice night
I'm stuffing a long woolen muffler
into this person's mouth

March 4, 2010

There Are Those Buddhists

like myself
who do not scorn the idea
of mere "things" possessing
a sanctity
of their own.

—John Blofeld
March 29, 2010

Unlimited Growth on a Planet of Finite Size

The brisk spring wind sets in motion the wheel
of mind restless as five monkeys
running in place

At least it's entertaining
when there are dreams of many

energetically bringing "Zen"

from India to China to Japan
to California and New York
riding on a wave of understanding

and like sunlight
arriving without a sound

April 3, 2010

"A Great Vampire Squid
Is Wrapped Around the Face of Humanity"

And no more "public" ownership of seeds
    which is as discouraging as the compost grinder
        disgorging sounds across the road like a semi truck

        Very pissed off turn on the jazz station really really loud
         possibly annoying another neighbor behind me

Remember before it all quickly drains away
    You were practicing "patience" today

April 21, 2010

Mocking Yourself

A night full of yellow rubber duckies
leads one to the low tide of the imagination
Actually someone's really out there
picking up sand dollars
after picking up the daily news

Yuk what a blast of the nasty past
with failing banks. Guess what?
you get no interest whatsoever
in this melancholy climate of late afternoon
For heaven's sake learn how to take care
of more than yourself
balancing the give and take of what it takes
to make a wholesome change into the American Dream
going south without a jot of understanding
about these phony wars and delirious debt

May 15, 2010

Wishing You Clear New Space Upon Your Departure

The space of course of foothills, mountains,
rivers, oceans and sky

And to rooms with all the books
And the voices that murmur them   all through time

And the meetings with old friends   and ones yet to arrive

Through the gates that open   to let you pass

May 28, 2010
for Leslie

Very Important & Natural
Absorbed in *People* Magazine
Beyond Giddy

What if every emotion has a self
—dozens of selves coming into and out of existence
none of them lasting very long
although seconds
can seem like total horrible eternity
Consider this—

"The thought is made in the mouth"
and action proceeds from immediate response—

"I was NOT on the phone with Genie for 30 minutes"
And to prove it I will throw this dishpan of water
on the newly lit stove.

Bit of a mess to clean up, but worth it
considering all the wet dust I found.

August 3, 2010

The Following Is Absolutely Free

Overcast and cool
it will be the equinox in a few weeks actually

"Ideological arrogance and willful ignorance
& incompetence compounded by cruelty"

are pre-existing conditions
that cause the red shafted flicker
to suddenly fly off
just like John Ashbery's poetry

We know who
put out the eyes of God
making justice blind
But we're not telling
for it might turn out very badly

for "us" in the long run
if we want to live a life of comfort
"we" must continue looking the other way

"Here have some of this enormously expensive whiskey"
it won't kill you right away"

Crash!   a glass is broken
in celebration
of a family party

One wonders

at the boundaries
of ownership

Probably celestial by now

September 8, 2010

Belongs to Everyone

Just read through my entire four years in the Japan Journal
It took about twenty minutes
And the incident I hope to find was never written down

"What color robes shall I wear?"
"Oh something to match your hair."

"Always now"
enjoying the moment

waiting for rain

which has already arrived

October 27, 2010
Thinking about Ko-san
(Morinaga Roshi)

Last Rays in the Garden

They lasted a long time didn't they

those rays

October 28, 2010

Overcast with the *SF Chronicle*

Reading the Datebook, the funnies

Sinking feeling
The echoing body

approaching the dark night of the year
like a movie thriller

Nix on one columnist, let's try another
For the sake of privacy from WikiLeaks
diplomats will get off the internet
says Jon Carroll
and meet in large parks
like Yosemite

Can you remember last night's social situation?
so worthlessly demanding and urgent

In Austria they loathe the death sentence
They don't want a Schwarzenegger museum
he put Tookie Williams to death in California

Twilight gets here so quickly

“This is my original, constant and true self”
upon seeing the morning star
on the 8th day of December

From here you begin

December 13, 2010

Active

As active
as an over-active imagination
—that's the wind
you're hearing now

This reflection is meant to be
refined by the simplest reduction

led by the voice of winter wind
reviewing history terribly old

A story is told in a single breath
so easy to remember
it blows right through you

December 29, 2010

Is This What Happened?

Just now
the plum blossoms
have arrived
near sunset
a dove lands
thru the silvery sky
of tomorrow's fog

Christopher Isherwood says
that Vivekananda says
there is no such thing as evil

like corporate sponsored democracy

"Emptiness" being the infinity of things

W.S. Merwin reads out at Commonweal Sunday afternoon
Lots of poets from out of town
Born in 1927, son of a Presbyterian minister
Refused to go to Trungpa's Halloween party

Lacy dark gothic clouds
race across a gold
full moon

Still at the kitchen sink
doing the dishes

400 BCE Ananda is asked
to "recite from memory
everything you heard
Gotama say."

Now year of the Iron Rabbit
a desperate focus
on "self" survival
—victims of independence
and freedom

"Why can't we do it
the way we USED to do it"

Found a pen
So much better now
Not as angry at the "consensus" president

And not cringing so much at the memory of my note
left on neighbor's car
"Park on your Own side of the road
—*The Owners* of this side of the road"

"The sympathetic gesture
the understanding smile
I wish we could but we can't
and it's not my fault"

Sounds
laden with rain the plum branch
breaks
as Caesar returns to Rome on the tube
in triumph

"Nothing must impede the nation's growth"

Four large tide surges

Sound on the page
Acoustical map. Sonic scoring.

"The heart is not an individual possession. It is not yours alone."
A deep and pervasive melancholy.

Tear yourself away

January–March 2011

Albert

When I came back from a trip to Europe and New York in the late '60s
I found the Summer of Love
and the Bay Area awash with psychedelic participants.

I went to visit Albert who was living in Mill Valley.
He showed me some new household practices he had learned.
When you are sweeping the floor in the morning,
take a piece of newspaper, dampen one edge
and lay it on the floor.
Then you sweep all the dust onto it and fold it up
put it neatly in the wastebasket.

And then I asked him, How can I understand this new hippie culture?
Albert said, Well, when you wake up in the morning, get stoned.
And I mean really really stoned.
If you do this every day
you can eventually change your consciousness.

About 15 years later when I saw him next
I asked, Did you ever say
when we were supposed to stop?

Albert Fairchild Saijo
February 4, 1926–June 2, 2011
June 15, 2011

"Write Something About Poetics"

I dream about a totem pole of poets.
Actually it was a poster Andrew Hoyem did
for a reading of Bolinas writers in the early '70s
at SFMOMA and we're sitting on each other's shoulders.

Now the local "wild" is looking pretty trimmed and tame

with "Extreme Conditions"
being the new weather norm.

Where did
all those late night thoughts go?
About Empitness

and "The Majority"
—being those who have "passed
away" from us—

I don't like the word "old"
when speaking about myself—
preferring the word "mature"

"She is in her mature years" watching

the great Blue
Heron strike a gopher in its hole
and gulp it down.

July 18, 2011

Dreaming Poets in Mexico with the *I Ching*
a Oaxaca Notebook
October 2011

October 4

Looking up at the sky from the patio
5100 feet above the sea
Wispy white clouds form
and reform, cluster into grey masses
The end of the rainy season
a possible abrupt downpour

Last night at a gathering of poets in Bolinas—
with Charles Olson
I'm to read one of his poems
but it's full of Polish names
I can't pronounce

October 5

It's not as if I was a wanderer—really holding to domestic stability
When the latter is a bit like holding onto a toothpick in the sea.
The trivial details of a new abode are absorbing for a while.
A shiny red plastic tray.
But the same person with the pen is still carried along.
And has lost her mind at the internet cafe trying to log on
to a crucially unfamiliar machine. Finds Ron Padgett
with news of Joe Brainard's *Collected Writing*;
Lyn Hejinian's *My Life* rescued from a pdf file;
publishers of Ed Dorn's *Bean News* looking for Joanna McClure.

And ants have joined me on the paper as I write.

Texas Governor, Rick Perry, suggest Mexico's drug wars may need
deployment of US Troops.
Mexico remembers the Mexican-American War. No way
for armed incursion.

This thing called "patience" as a practiced virtue results in a clear
unmolested mind.
Random opening to the *I Ching* #56 The Wanderer—
"Persistently conscious of being a stranger in a strange land—"

Thursday October 6

Dreams are full of parties and social situations, faces half-familiar,
    wanting to be chased, out of the reality of the moment.
    I have no place to sleep says a confused young man.
    Here take this mattress on my bedroom floor.

Clinging to brightness, depending on nature in its radiance,
the strength within "refuses to be burnt out."
A voluntary dependence on, say
        the sun in its early morning concentration.

The setting sun, of what I like to call "Mega Maturity"
can impel one to uninhibited celebration—"to enjoy life while it lasts."
Otherwise the lamentation of age—
            "Lucky you to have lasted so long"—
Understanding the grief of passing with clarity
                    gives every moment a monumental heart

Friday October 7

Over the right shoulder   sun rises
through a rooftop planter of waving reeds.

Like Graciela Iturbide's photograph "Jardin de Fierro"
—rebar planted in cement
building hopes for the future.

Departing in a few moments for the Llano Park weekly market,
walking the street north outside the door.
I can move faster on busy Oaxaca streets
by lengthening my stride
lengthen the stride.

Saturday October 8

"Mexico needs no enemies with friends
like the US Bureau of Alcohol Tobacco & Firearms"

US federal agents conceived operations
which has Mexico's "bad guys" well armed and arrogant.
"The ATF is there to impede,
yet seems to supervise gun running into Latin America."

October 12

Every morning the sidewalks we walk on
are swept into neat piles
of dust and debris. And left there.
Until wind and the day disperse them.

The incredible varied song from a neighbor's bird
whose cage is brought outside every afternoon
for the air.

There's the gecko doing its pushups on the cement block wall—

Dreadful concepts like "developing nations"
Look around, at least 10,000 years in this valley
of continuous living, culture, history.

Who rang the door bell?

October 13

I'm traveling in a car with Allen Ginsberg. We stop
at this mysterious wooded place, primeval twisted trees.

An owl lands on my shoulder.
I'm taken for a ceremonial bathing by some women
Everyone is very gentle. I find my clothes.
We must get back, says Allen. The car needs to be fixed.
We're still deep in the forest.
You need a licensed driver, says Jack.

A great mood is infectious. Friendship, a real winner.
Frivolous celebrations are just idle pleasures
for an empty heart, and believe you me,
indulgence is no way, in the long run,
enjoyable.

Sunday October 16

A week ago a "relic" from the late Polish Pope John Paul II
was brought to the main cathedral on the Oaxaca zocalo.
Thousands lined up to see it.
The newspaper, somewhat confusingly,
has pictures of the Pope in his casket with a glass top,
laid out in all his ceremonial
robes of red and black and gold.
Like he's newly dead.

I find out today that the Pope
was a life size replica made of wax.

And after musing about what part of the body
could be contained in the reliquary
(I mean, what is left after the decay of the flesh but hair, fingernails, teeth, bone)

someone in the "know" told me it was a vial of blood.
One of the four taken from his body
for possible transfusions
during his last days in 2005.

The blood in an elaborate silver reliquary
will be taken on a pilgrimage around Mexico until December.

The first stop, of course
—the Basilica of Our Lady of Guadalupe
in Mexico City
"Empress of the Americas"

Tuesday October 18

Help! The ridge pole sags to the breaking point
because the ends are too weak
for the load they bear.

A solution must be found as quickly as possible,
but one must be extraordinarily cautious.
And join with the populace, for the possibility
of rescuing the "whole".

"That good and right may prevail, one may give up one's life.
There are more important things than life."
says "the Preponderance of the Great."

The large blind guy is standing in the entrance doorway to the studios.
"I live here" I say in English. He lets me pass.
His two collared and splendid looking cats,
stand in the walkway behind him.

A tiny tiny bubble floats through the window and now sits on my finger.
Reflects the photographer who takes the picture.

Hey Thanks

Took me one and half hours to write
"Just This"

Adapt

to the times
and you will have listeners
all of them equally cynical
as you are. "Beyond
the Missouri Sky" plays
under Oaxaca rain
clouds the issue. Looking at the tissue silk
of a tiny handkerchief made
in Japan before "the war".
Which war, one wonders now looking
under Fujiyama's
snow capped peak.
Everything seems a peaceful treasure
like this moment when voices
arrive beyond the gate
and then evaporate.

October 17, 2011
Oaxaca

Poem Beginning with a Line by Philip Lamantia

"A sibilant declaration that 'life'
is contained in the mystic illumination
of the glorious page."
No matter that the blind man, our neighbor
fills the entrance with Spanish
his two sleek cats backing
him up all the way to Malaga
where Islamic energies mingled well
with those who conquered Mexico
At least that's what Philip told me—
Aren't those codices the story
of a crushed past
on a piece of old bark cloth
ready to flash a DNA of color coded light
in an instant revelation of the past?

Sylvan witches masquerading as historians
flop out a piece of geography
and all of a sudden you have ancestors!
Hiding out on a sun bleached sheet of cloth
protected by blankets of enigma
and a spiritscape from the moon.

October 17 / November 8, 2011
—for Cedar Sigo

Wild Current Is Blooming Pink
the Odyssey Found at Random

You are in search of some simple way to find your home
but the old gods reach out with their stories and resentments
and so your journey will be troublesome
and, frankly, endless
for you will go on to meet people
who have never heard of you

Caught inland
by the outgoing long tide

Where you will find a place to plant some seeds
And tell your story all over again

And give a bit of sacrifice
so those dead ones
can speak again

February 18, 2012

Take a Deep Breath

Can't seem to get the fire
started this morning need to add dreams
so flames rise quick as thoughts
and drift out
into the overcast sky
Mind here and now
is Buddha says Dogen

Appearing in front of the bright and temporal poppies
about to open against the perfume
of a small gold narcissus

Just searching for information from the air
waves a gentle moment from tiny plum leaves
the day with barely an adieu

March 22, 2012

Early Breakfast with Mourning Dove

See what happens when you waddle around
beneath the bird seed table
waiting for a hand out
You've become a sitting duck   a pile of tiny grey feathers

March 27, 2012

Everything I Know About You Guys Is Wrong

Exhausting the intellect and imagination
what is left?

The flicker walks on the grass
and then freezes still
as do I—

This is a chance to practice "meditation"

He's my teacher
listening to worms turning

In a "dry and merciless reality"

"You" are what remains

March 30, 2012

Can You Believe

Can you believe the amount of global war
we are more
than halfway into?

And now we can't use computers
since "they" spy on you
and space is no longer free

Recollections of those stories
about selling apples
and pencils
for dimes and dances

And then warned about future

dismal prospects
of ambitious development
of waterless open spaces

I do care if you know I'm here
behind the closed doors of security
heart beating like a beast

terrified at the futility of control

based on the perpetual goal
of optimum growth
intrinsically wrong
on a finite fly specked planet

Here's looking at you!

June 1, 2012

Barely Viewed Lunar Eclipse

Here I was feeling so sad for my neighbor the botanist
          who died alone in the hospital
but it turns out his children and most recent wife were actually there,
                although he wasn't conscious
He was known as the Wood Pig among his Mayan workers

So a friend and I went down to the beach to burn some incense for him
but it was so windy we went up a wooded trail
and made a little altar sweeping away the pine needles
leaving roses, three cherries, plus two Mexican oak leaves from his garden
with four sticks of burning incense

The Monterey pine tree above had a very camouflaged
heart shaped stone pushed into the bark

                                        The full moon 3am last Monday
                                Kind of empty across the road now
                          in this morning's reflection
                  now the center of that little green empire is gone

Wednesday
June 6, 2012

"Nobody Told Me Grief Felt So Much Like Fear"

—*C.S. Lewis*

Distress, tension, mental pain, hostility
One can barely spell them out

"I must control my destiny"

Go ahead

and visit the old homes, the old graves—
creaky ancestors from the south.

Come out from that ground-in position
on a scruffy wild coast north

Remember to surrender
is to survive

(At least when you're 18
like my grandfather
and the Other Side wins)

Does this really work?

A sharp-shinned hawk stuns himself
banging into the glass door

Instantaneous arising and passing
Waking up
from a dream of isolation

"There's no way of telling people
that they are all walking around
shining like the sun"

They just won't believe
they're missing so much.

June 18, 2012

Romantic

Half human half bird

and a headdress of crazy colored feathers

Careful steps
to bring in the sun's
pale silk of the summer's new year

stitched with meadow wild flowers

finally a breath

moves around the garden

recognize me?

July 21, 2012

Make Yourself at Home in the Dreamy Bardo

Which story are you trying to tell—
the one about when he lived in a chicken house
and boosted twinkies from the market?

The far off flicker sounds
after a stormy morning
And you are ready with your mind
wandering epic
from a damp musty room
trying to tie a microphone
to a common ear
Where was it they first met?
besides on the page, I mean
Inside the wind's heat?
Shh! don't say anything he said as he kissed her.
People were circling the bed
in the middle of the room. Take heart
she said. Would you like
some company? he replied

Outside the war was still active
like when hasn't it been.
The apples slowly ripened
just ahead
of the fawn's open mouth

The memories weren't needed anymore
they were on their own
—really the faintest ink holds the best memories
and passage from mind to page
is frankly open

December 2, 2012

The Epic of World Mythology

"This is our homeland. All this is our homeland."
And here, the priests are in control of the elements.

But then there was a long long drought and no one could bring rain.
So there were no crops, nothing to eat, and the people left.

Sometime after, big storm came
and made the world's biggest natural disaster.
Then the Giant Asian Hornet arrived in France
hidden inside a delivery
of Chinese pottery

Some animals don't want to move
The deer here spend all their lives
in a two mile radius—
the back yard is ankle deep in pellet poo
They are practically domesticated.

Rescue honey bee from downing in rain water
cover it with jasmine
but it dies in the night
near dawn on my 78th birthday. Allen and Peter
dressed in Indian white give me an embrace
then sit down to a meal
covered with a clean cotton napkin

Drive to watch the elephant seals in Drakes Bay cove
enormous and territorial on a beach the size of a table cloth.

The deer eat the fallen yellow apple leaves like potato chips
—"they must get *something* out of them"

A poet reminds us "The book is breath"
in the very very far west

December 26, 2012

"God" as a Man-Made Arrangement

Hurtling towards the dark fog, the overcast
hoping the book will open the door to familiar recognition

The emotional life of animals—
Not so long ago it was said they had no "feelings"
no consciousness. All was human projection.

"The first storm wetted the earth
The second storm soaked it"

Wander through pathways of wind visiting ancestors
on a rainy night, into violent stirrings searching
for a story to retell. Forget the heroic voyage
in a remodeled modern world.
A wandering epic of childhood insecurities
blackmailing the stars.

The big doe chases her youngest away.

Here's the sun broke through the lousy world debt
illuminating equally lousy investments
that work out extra great

if calamity occurs. There goes
the morning sun behind the neighbor's killer pine.

The ashes need to be cleaned out of the stove.

December 27, 2012

Seeing the Old Year Out

Good lord all this teetering on the new definition of "edge"
How will we ever get in
and out of town when the sea rises
through the marshy end of the lagoon.
Exiled through the change
of governments bought and sold
by words too shrewd to evaluate

Remember how the heart is always located
by its place in the body, by the bottom of a mountain, on the slopes to the sea

Watching it all go by as if owned by no one,
the watcher sneezes and disappears

momentarily.
She is forced to watch from behind a curtain
She can't go out by herself
to see the red starfish

Longing for the elixir of movement

now that we're a year older

So open your book and dream what is written

December 30, 2012

It's the Big Trip

Anselm doesn't really want to leave
says his daughter

But there he goes
a bull's eye flight
just after full moon rises

You really don't want to be "elsewhere"
when this here
is so perfectly loving
and familiar

January 29, 2013
Anselm Hollo
April 12, 1934–January 29, 2013

"Finger Pointing at the Moon Is Not the Moon"

Say goodnight

to the small field of daffodils
while doves and sparrows
pass overhead

Stars as grand citizens of the sky
appear near dazzled moon
Still possible to read
under its full light

The doors of the little palace open
messages go out
What happened last night?

It was that meteor flashing
like a runaway gazelle
down the coast.

April 27, 2013
day after Peter Warshall's Passing

Stoutly Maintains I Never Rewrite

So what about those many sheets of drifting time
and intents
hoping to "pin down"
the illusive tone
that makes a poem

Peripheral, from the sidelines
looking in from the edge
Always give yourself a quick
escape route
at assemblies of people
sit near an exit
be on the fringe
able to drift away

from the front and center
places where power
plays a dangerous role

on earth the only place
we *can* live

Head full of spring wind's pollen
"self radicalized" through random reading
Did you do this to me?

April 29, 2013

Old Bird's Dream

A 62 year old albatross named Wisdom gave birth
to healthy chick on February 3 this year
—maybe raised 32 so far

"I've grown used to the idea
that everything around me
in nature
happens unobserved
and unrecorded"

"It takes a lot to straighten out the record"

Think of dream as autobiographical episodes
common and creative
Recall dreamtime dimensions
of contacting ancestors
who send gifts of songs,
stories, designs
Turn illusion into luminosity
Bring back milkweed
to 120 million acres

of poisoned farm land

Let the monarchs fly

April 30, 2013

After Having My Teeth Cleaned

Day after day, they're numbered.
Even if you live in the "now".

I don't want to pursue you
if you don't think this way.

but really, how else can you make history

unless you see time pass by
with its chronology
of cause and effect.

A large willow branch breaks in the wind.
Now cut into pieces

to burn when it dries

during this summer's
cold mornings.

May 17, 2013

Almost a Quiet Room

Almost international and almost local
a fire is started in the stove
the last of May

Are you awake?   Yes I am.

Is everything still about "You"?

Why don't you listen?
Are you hard of hearing?

Waiting for that old inner peace.

yuk   fuck it

May 29, 2013

"If Your Body Is Ill, Your Mind Needn't Be"

Joanna McClure can't remember Emily Dickinson's name
and tells me what Jess Collins used to say—

"At your age, do you ever think about the hereafter?"

"Yes. When I go into another room and ask myself
'what am I here after?'"

August 4, 2013

Better Get Wise Again

-1-

Be in awe of the tiny things under your paws.
A bit angry. Why wasn't I told?

Who "owns" memories, anyway.   Are we finished yet?
"Everything" is poetry, animated, kicking its heels.

Squabble during supper over who gets to tell the story—
you keep INTERRUPTING me—
Dinner guest is charmed, I'm sure.
Thank William Carlos Williams.

-2-

The last day before the New Year melancholic,
with very shitty grass
causing anxiety over duplicity of self—a powerless funk
over predatory capitalism. With its security hypes.
Becoming intoxicated on New Year's eve I vow
to be more modest. Apologies never cut the cake.

-3-

We need more action here.
Cook some white beans and ham.

Meta data hanging on a pig's thigh
connected to the global air. Does it give you pleasure?

-4-

Sailing under the Golden Gate cool on a cool day
cast over with tremulous news.

The doctor got tired of listening to her
Am I okay? she said,   as he walked out the door.

-5-

Summer is finally here and it's January
on the North Coast—along with the new "intelligence"
of climate in what we call "our" environment

-6-

Drought time…
150 household gallons per day
Try drinking that much.

Renew your passport. Bend over.
This won't take a minute.

-7-

Within the "Poetics of Interconnectedness"
the morning sun appears over the rim of a book.

The world seen as object and story—

constant online reassurances that one exists
—constant management of self.

December 2013–January 2014

Post Extinction

How could you forget me so quickly—

But the way you are reached, touched, awakened
by the world continues

the same way you yourself
pass along a freely given
lineage of existence

Each one, every thing, perfect "as is"

Like the moon
going down
never really leaves the sky

So "existence" never quits,
never began,   never ended

You see in the moment
So sorry it will never be

like this again—

But when has the present ever been singular?

Everything with a language of distinction

with sorrow, with melancholy
with sweet appreciation

of an extinguished future

when water becomes
a state of being

September 2014

ABOUT THE AUTHOR

One of the major women poets of the SF Renaissance, Joanne Kyger was born in 1934 in Vallejo, CA. After studying at UC Santa Barbara, she moved to San Francisco in 1957, where she became a member of the circle of poets around Jack Spicer and Robert Duncan. In 1960, she and then-husband Gary Snyder traveled in Japan and India where, along with Allen Ginsberg and Peter Orlovsky, they met the Dalai Lama. She returned to California in 1964 and published her first book, *The Tapestry and the Web*, in 1965. In 1969, she settled in Bolinas, where she continues to reside today. She has published over 30 books of poetry and prose, including *Strange Big Moon, The Japan and India Journals: 1960-1964* (2000), *As Ever: Selected Poems* (2002), and *About Now: Collected Poems* (2007), which won the 2008 Josephine Miles Award from PEN Oakland.

www.ingramcontent.com/pod-product-compliance
Lightning Source LLC
Jackson TN
JSHW061647170426
101040JS00018B/402
* 9 7 8 0 8 7 2 8 6 6 8 0 5 *